MW00937152

EXPECT THE UNEXPECTED

Finding Opportunity in Unexpected Business Results

RICHARD PARSONS

Archway Publishing books may be ordered through booksellers or by contacting:

Archway Publishing
1663 Liberty Drive
Bloomington, IN 47403
www.archwaypublishing.com
844-669-3957

ISBN: 978-1-6657-0770-1 (sc)
ISBN: 978-1-6657-0771-8 (e)

Library of Congress Control Number: 2021911053

Print information available on the last page.

Archway Publishing rev. date: 6/22/2021

CONTENTS

INTRODUCTION

He who would search for pearls must dive below.
—John Dryden

As a young business executive, I attended a training course where the coach shared a Chinese proverb that really made me think. I had been focused on creating strategic and operational plans for business units and had focused on critical success factors specific to each business. We were convinced that if we achieved these critical success factors, the business would achieve success, grow, and make money. And if we did not achieve these, then the business would result in failure. For example, in a rice business we owned, we felt we needed to establish an instant rice product to compete with the number two business in the segment. In addition, we had some stagnant brands that we felt needed some significant investment in order for them to grow. We also planned on making a few strategic acquisitions.

The Chinese proverb went something like this:

A farmer had only one horse. One day, his horse ran away.

His neighbors said, "I'm so sorry. This is such bad news. You must be so upset."

The man just said, "Good news, bad news—who knows?"

A few days later, his horse came back with twenty wild horses following. The man and his son corralled all twenty-one horses.

His neighbors said, "Congratulations! This is such good news. You must be so happy!"

The man just said, "Good news, bad news—who knows?"

One of the wild horses kicked the man's only son, breaking both his legs.

His neighbors said, "I'm so sorry. This is such bad news. You must be so upset."

The man just said, "Good news, bad news—who knows?"

The country went to war, and every able-bodied young man was drafted to fight. The war was terrible and killed every young man, but the farmer's son was spared since his broken legs prevented him from being drafted.

His neighbors said, "Congratulations! This is such good news. You must be so happy!"

The man just said, "Good news, bad news—who knows?"

I was left a little anxious and reflective. If we couldn't really comprehend what was good and what was bad, then our plans were nothing more than pipe dreams. Of course I gained composure and convinced myself that the real world was not as complicated as the parable implied. While occasionally things went wrong, we certainly know what is *usually* good and *usually* bad.

As I considered our activities, all our research, debate, and thought, I was confident that we could put together a great plan. In fact, the new products, improved brands, and new acquisitions on which we were focusing incredible energy and resources were sure to be winners and drive the business forward! Now, twenty years later, I look back and see that the instant rice, the supported brands, and the acquisitions were maybe only mildly or partially successful. They really didn't amount to much more than a little blip, or on occasion a little dip, in the overall business performance.

A serious disruption will happen in every business; it's not a question of *if* but *when*. If the disruption is big enough, it can destroy you, but it can also give you the opportunity to succeed far beyond your previous achievements. No one predicted the major impact of the COVID-19 pandemic, but it has destroyed some companies (restaurants) and helped others (Zoom).

I have since seen many examples where business executives do all the right things, but the results end up totally wrong. I've also seen executives do all the wrong things, but the businesses thrive! In truth, it is not always about the clever business executive; we are always playing the odds against unknown and unexpected events. The world *is* very complicated, and often, there is a new, unseen Netflix just around the corner. So whatever grand plans and efforts we implement for Blockbuster won't really matter. Remember what your grandfather told you: "Don't count your chickens before they hatch." Lots of eggs means you have a lot of eggs—not a lot of chickens. And don't put all your eggs in one basket. The conventional wisdom was built on the understanding that we really never know something is a sure thing. This is true, so why do so many businesspeople do exactly the opposite: find a "sure" thing and get excited or indifferent before things mature and either get all in or all out as quickly as possible?

In the world of statistics and probabilities, the mathematicians solve this problem by adding an error term into the equation. Mathematical exercises are not particularly helpful ways for a businessperson to manage the unexpected events they will encounter. However, there are ways to prepare for and deal with surprises in business. There are strategies that allow us to respond to and stay on top of the turbulent waves rather than be sucked under.

This book will take us through some short case studies that exemplify how to deal with surprising situations. We can learn many things from understanding the principle of unknown factors and surprises in business. This book will also discuss business approaches we can implement, which will help us deal with these issues. Three of the major discussion points will be:

1. Stay flexible and keep necessary reserves.

2. Be close to the customer. We often focus on our competitors and worry about surprises from them, but more often than not, it is the customer who surprises us. Customer tastes and preferences can change quickly, sinking a promising business move. This is a particular problem for successful companies that believe their success is a vindication of their approach, and they continue on the same path even though the market has changed.

3. Focus on what you can control. Especially in the short term, don't expect things to turn out like you planned. Owners and executives can get caught up with enthusiasm or despair over short-term results and lose discipline and direction.

On the surface, these ideas seem pretty simple, but that is exactly what makes them so powerful. It is the simple stuff that we don't get completely right that gets us into trouble. You have to get the fundamentals right; otherwise, all the fancy stuff you put on top of it will just add confusion. Keeping things appropriately simple is the foundation upon which the other ideas will succeed.

In our rice business, we had a salesman showing us a complicated and sophisticated MRP system. This computer system would manage the parts and in-process inventory needed to bring the final product together as scheduled. The salesman told us what impressive results it had achieved with defense contractors and automobile companies—companies that had thousands of critical parts to assemble and manage. We looked the salesman in the eye and pointed out that we put rice in a box. It was not exactly what he wanted to hear, but it did keep us grounded in our reality and our own specific critical success factors.

Another example of making things too hard occurred when I was a junior consultant. I was working on an order and delivery system for the Saudi Arabian Oil Company. We were building a custom computer program to track the orders and deliveries against those orders. It was a multimillion-dollar project, and this was many years ago, so in today's terms, it would have been even bigger. Our client had endless buckets full of money, and cost was no object, so we built them the most sophisticated custom computer system that could be built. After a few weeks of working on the project, I finally understood enough about it to ask appropriate questions. I learned that the orders to be processed were for oil tankers. Now, that's a big order and worth tracking. But then I found out that they only shipped one tanker a week. *A sophisticated computer system to manage one order a week?* I could easily keep that on a three-by-five notecard. Need a backup? Make a copy. Worried about fire? Keep a copy off-site. In fact, I can come up with a lot more things that could go wrong with a computer system for keeping track of such a simple process than you could for an old-fashioned paper log.

So, let's go ahead and look at the examples in this book.

SECTION I

CHAPTER 1

Stay Flexible

It is not the strongest of the species that survives,
nor the most intelligent that survives. It is the
one that is the most adaptable to change.
—Charles Darwin

In today's world, external forces are rapidly changing. This is true in terms of technology, customer preferences, competitive entities, regulation, and globalization. Internal factors are also rapidly changing, including employee demographics, resource availability, regulations, and motivations. All of this has created an unprecedented level of uncertainty and risk. Reeves and Deimler said, "Since 1980 the volatility of business operating margins, largely static since the 1950s, has more than doubled, as has the size of the gap between winners (companies with high operating margins) and losers (those with low ones.)" This fact, coupled with the general inaccuracy of forecasts, requires that businesses be prepared to adapt quickly and effectively. If it were not for the unexpected, a chief executive officer of a successful company would have an easy job, simply keep things going the way they are. But things don't stay the same; there are both external and internal surprises to which the executive must respond.

At the beginning of every strategic plan or operation plan, there is usually a section forecasting the economy and the operating environment. I have always included these in any business plan. However, the one thing we know about forecasts is that they are always wrong. Why start the plan with something that is wrong? You may say the economy will grow at 3 percent, that competitors will attempt to expand into your region, or other such things that are critically important to your plans. But once again, even if you rely on a blue-chip panel of economist and the latest and greatest statistical techniques, the forecasts will be wrong.

How accurate are forecasts?

A KPMG survey of more than 540 senior executives of large businesses showed that over a recent five-year period, only 1 percent of firms have hit forecasts—and just 22 percent have come within 5 percent either way. On average, forecasts have been off by 13 percent. Executives have estimated that such errors have removed 6 percent from their firms' values. So, if they are so bad and so important, something must be done. There are only two things that can be done: figure out how to improve forecasting with investing in better data and resources and develop the ability to flexibly respond to missed forecast.

Any business plan is faced with changes that it has no way of anticipating. New competitors emerge, technology changes, and consumers' tastes evolve—and all of this happens at warp speed. Plans must not lock you in; every business needs options. Given the need to respond to change, you need to realize the business itself must change.

Amy Gallo gives some ideas on how to make your business plan a living document that can change as needed. She suggests:

1. Focus on your largest asset.
2. Describe tests ventures to determine the best way forward.
3. Include risk assessment and contingencies.
4. Revisit the plan often.

I would point out that in focusing on your largest asset, perhaps it is better to think about focusing on your largest asset of the future. The pen we house our dinosaurs in may be our largest asset, but it could become a millstone around our necks. What asset is growing and what assets will emerge as the critical assets for the future?

On the issues of test ventures, one must also be careful not to throw away the baby with the bathwater. I have seen many companies get excited about growing through new products only to neglect their core products. The case study on Home Depot in this book describes the successful growth in a new business (contractors) that some felt left the core business neglected. Sometimes consumer product companies try to add 5 percent by focusing on a new product or variant—only to see the 95 percent suffer. In a way, the Twix advertising example in this book shows the focus on new with neglect of the core. The best test ventures explore the areas where things are rapidly changing (technology, consumer tastes, and business environment) and allow the company to be prepared to adapt ahead of its competitors.

J. D. Meier said, "One of the best ways to get results is to change your approach. You can change yourself faster than you can change other people. This gives you incredible flexibility in any situation." And it is true for the individual and true for business.

Academic research on the subject of strategic flexibility has conceptualized the following issues:

1. Strategic flexibility is built with excess resources.
2. Strategic flexibility is enhanced by decreasing dependence on assets that are already in place.
3. Strategic flexibility requires the ability to replicate core skills and abilities across divisions and operations.
4. Strategic flexibility is the ability to exercise incremental options, including experiments, as discussed above.
5. Strategic flexibility is the ability to reallocate resources quickly and efficiently in response to change.
6. Strategic flexibility requires the ability to modify relationships, contracts, and alliances.
7. Strategic flexibility requires increases in effective communication.

Recognize that no company operates in a vacuum or as an island. You are part of a supply chain, part of a consumer environment, part of a competitive environment, and part of a macroeconomic environment. You must have contacts and be close to each of these areas to pick up and interpret the signals coming from each of your critical relationships. Who are the key people in your company who will receive and interpret the information coming out of these channels? Will they recognize the critical information? Do you need to increase resources in any of these touch points so that you have the information you need to plan, react, and execute per the constantly changing environment?

Rely on data rather than intuition whenever you can. Too many managers think they know the answers and have some special understanding of the marketplace and the consumer. Relying on data rather than your gut will make you seem like a genius even though it is really the most basic business 101. No responsible company would fund a major advertising campaign before they tested it with target consumers—even if the CEO loves the campaign.

Experiments, as discussed above, require funding. And since, by definition, many experiments fail, management should recognize the need to fund failures. Since the purpose of experimentation is to learn, a failed experiment may in fact produce the most valuable information. If necessary, increase your cost of capital to allow an additional sector of experimental failures. An alternative approach is to have an experimental division, which is just a cost center, which can then work on spending the allocated funds in the most effective way rather than trying to earn short-term profits.

The greater uncertainty that a business is faced with, the more reserves the business should keep. Since uncertainty often takes a negative toll on reserves, the reserves must be put in place in advance. This will allow for response and change when the need arises. These reserves can come in a wide variety of resources other than just cash. A key resource to consider is human resources. A salesperson who knows a particular channel or market may be critical to a new venture. A scientist who understands a particular product may be critical in adapting to changes. If we thin down our employment force to the bare minimum, we do not have the ability to react efficiently to change that is thrust upon us. Cash reserves can usually be met with borrowing capabilities. Ford made good use of reserves in 2009 when GM and Chrysler suffered a bankruptcy and a government takeover. Ford was able to stop short of the cliff. Ford had strategically set up a significant line of credit by mortgaging its factories, equipment, and assets in 2006, and it was able to raise $18 billion and thereby avoid the government bailout. This provided a huge boost in consumer and investor views of Ford. The company's stock went up by more than a factor of six times in the six years that followed the crisis.

For references and additional reading, see Sources.

CHAPTER 2

Turning Waste to Gold

If you want to succeed, you should strike out on new paths,
rather than travel the worn paths of accepted success.

—John D. Rockefeller

Topics

- Disruptive innovation
- External threats

Discussion Questions

- Was it a worthwhile strategy for Mr. Rockefeller to try to attack the new electric power as unsafe?
- How risky are R&D investments? Do you need to be a big successful company to make them? Was the

investment in trying to find an alternative use for gasoline risky?

- What if electric cars had become standard instead of gasoline-powered vehicles? What other options did Standard Oil have?

By some accounts, John D. Rockefeller was the richest man who ever lived. Yet in the middle of his success, he was faced with the same kind of disruptive innovation that destroyed the horse and buggy industry! His wealth, power, and influence were based on the fact that he had established a virtual monopoly in the oil industry. At that time, the oil industry meant kerosene! Kerosene was used to light the homes and streets of the nation. During the Civil War, the supply of southern turpentine—and even the whale oil business—were disrupted, leading to strong demands for kerosene. The rise of the kerosene industry eventually brought about the downfall of the whale oil business, which had previously been used as the primary source of lighting. Kerosene soon became the fuel of choice, lighting the city, the farm, and industry and "extending the day for the nation." And John D. Rockefeller was king of it all.

He once said of his critics whom he felt were in the way of his progress, "Of course it is natural that the man who drove the stagecoach should be antagonistic to the railroad." Yet he would soon have to learn this lesson himself and manage his own transformation away from kerosene.

Rockefeller's source of power, wealth, and influence was tied to kerosene, and all of it was now threated. In 1882, Thomas Edison established a company to compete with the established gas lighting utilities. As the market expanded and electric lighting began to replace kerosene, Edison and Nikola Tesla would compete over using AC or DC current. However their battle, the "Battle of the Currents," would not really slow down the rapid expansion of electric lights throughout America. Tesla's work would underpin the rise of Westinghouse, and Thomas Edison's work eventually resulted in General Electric. As a result of the rise of electric lighting, Rockefeller and his business empire were threatened. The new technology, the wave of the future, was electricity. Edison and Tesla both had major backers. Edison had J. P. Morgan financing him, and Tesla was associated with George Westinghouse.

What could Rockefeller do? The natural response would be to fight against the new technology. The first thing he did was try to slow down increasing use of electricity for lighting. There was considerable fear over this new unseen power source. He tried to encourage the fear and thereby slow down the new technology. He had become the embodiment of the stagecoach man fighting the rise of the railroad. As it became apparent this would not work he searched for a new approach.

A quote often attributed to John D. Rockefeller is this: "If you want to succeed, you should strike out on new paths, rather than travel the worn paths of accepted success." Putting his money where his mouth was, he directed his research scientist to find uses for the by-products of his refining process. As kerosene was distilled, it produced other petroleum products in the process, one of which was gasoline. Gasoline was a waste product and discarded. As a result of this work by Rockefeller and others, many new products were developed, including paraffin wax, Vaseline, roofing and road-covering tar, and even chewing gum. And even though electric lighting was growing rapidly and cutting into kerosene profits, Rockefeller's business continued to find success in everything else, including heating oil, varnish, and lubricants.

In the early 1880 and 1890s, German engineers experimented with simple gasoline engines on bicycles, and Henry Ford developed a prototype automobile that traveled a rapid thirty miles per hour. These engines ran on gasoline, one of the byproducts of kerosene manufacturing, and Rockefeller sent representatives to these events with great interest.

In 1896, Henry Ford produced his first experimental automobile powered by gasoline. By 1920, there were nine million vehicles on the road in the United States. This, of course, would be the future engine of the Rockefeller empire. And it is quite ironic that Henry Ford was the chief engineer for Edison Illumination Company, the thorn in Rockefeller's side, when he built his experimental car—and Ford continued his work with encouragement from Edison.

The rapid development of major industrial enterprises during this golden age of capitalism encouraged and supported each other. The railroads made Rockefeller's monopoly possible, and the automobile gave it a second and resurgent life. The rapid growth of the automobile did not automatically default to the need for gas. Many engines at this time ran on alcohol. Ford said alcohol was "a cleaner, nicer, better fuel for automobiles than gasoline."

During the development of the automobile, petroleum had an advantage over alcohol because of a heavy tax on alcohol, which had been passed to pay for the Civil War and was intended as a sin tax targeted at beverages, but no exceptions had been written in for other alcohol uses. When Congress attempted to consider a "free alcohol" bill, the Rockefellers squarely opposed the bill and helped keep the tax on their potential competitor. Finally, in 1906, Congress lifted the alcohol tax, but by that time, the new Texas oil fields were driving the price of oil down and limiting the opportunities for manufactured alcohol to be a gasoline substitute. Rockefeller's Standard Oil could now be pulled along by the rapid expansion of automobiles, which more than covered the decline in kerosene sales.

Rockefeller's early success continued on through the challenge from electric lighting. Even after the antitrust breakups, the spin-off companies continued to grow, and his wealth increased. The spin-off companies include many of today's most powerful companies, including Conoco, Chevron, Exxon, and Mobil.

For references and additional reading, see Sources.

CHAPTER 3

An Idea without a Home

An invasion of armies can be resisted, but
not an idea whose time has come.

—Victor Hugo

Topics

- Innovation
- Teamwork
- Patience
- Synergies
- Corporate culture

Discussion Questions

- When you pitch an idea for a long time, and nothing comes of it, when is it time to move on?
- How can a company obtain cross-fertilization of ideas?

There are many examples of accidental discoveries, including penicillin and the telephone. There are also examples of failed inventions that found a fortuitous alternative use, including Viagra. Pfizer's Viagra sells almost $2 billion a year, but it was originally a failed attempt at a cardiovascular drug designed to treat angina. Male test subjects noticed a certain side effect—and, well, the rest is history. Many of these "failure" lessons are rooted in science and innovation; when looking from a business standpoint, perhaps the best example is that of Post-it notes.

The iconic Post-it note was originally a failed idea, and then it took many years to actually make it. This is especially significant because 3M has long had a stellar reputation for innovation by incorporating innovation as one of its critical success factors. Recently, in a survey of corporate leaders, 3M was voted as the number three innovation leader behind Apple and Google. 3M's keys to innovation success are outlined by Fred Palensky, their chief technology officer. He believes that culture—more than organization—allows for open sharing of ideas. This culture embodies a view that technologies have no boundaries or ownership and are therefore available to any business or industry within 3M around the world. 3M also is famous for allowing employees to spend 15 percent of their time on their own research interests outside of their normal job duties.

For a company that was focused so much on innovation, Post-it Notes had quite a difficult road to success, suffering setback after setback. Way back in 1968, Dr. Spencer Silver, a new research scientist at 3M's central research labs, was looking for "a bigger, stronger, tougher adhesive." He failed. His failure was a weak adhesive that was pressure sensitive and could be removed and reapplied without leaving a residue. He thought he had something, but he didn't know what it could be used for. In his words, he had the "solution," but he just didn't know what problem it would solve yet! What a backward approach to the normal process of discovery where the problem at hand usually directs the efforts. Dr. Silver went on a campaign explaining his discovery to other employees of 3M, even conducting seminars. This was not just one or two times. He spent five years pushing and believing in the value of his idea before he got a hit. Within a corporate environment, this shows true persistence and a committed belief in innovation and ideas—on Dr. Silver's part *and* on the part of 3M, which was funding the time and effort.

Usually businesses require a more immediate payback, or at least a clear plan to move forward into revenue-producing products before they will continue to support an idea. It is normal in a business to require a five-year plan and insist that ideas go through a whole series of higher-up approvals. Dr. Silver had to believe enough in the product's potential that he would stake his time and reputation on it, and 3M had to believe enough in its scientist that it would support him in doing so.

The problem that the new adhesive could solve was finally discovered by Arthur Fry, of the New Product Development division. He had attended one of Dr. Silver's seminars and though of the adhesive one night while participating in his church choir. He was having problems with the little pieces of paper he used to mark the correct pages in his church choir hymnal. He realized that Dr. Silver's adhesive could solve his problem. Arthur had worked with 3M for about twenty years already, and he understood how 3M wanted to cross-fertilize ideas. He had no problem "bootlegging" the idea to move it forward.

Even though 3M encouraged its employees to talk to other departments and share ideas, it still took five years for Dr. Silver's failure to find a problem to which it could "stick." Most businesses would have "archived" the idea long before this. If you enjoy Post-it Notes today, then you can thank the open, innovative, and supportive culture of 3M.

Even though the solution now had a problem to solve, there were still the whole slew of business problems to overcome. The product was originally introduced in 1977 as "Press 'n Peel," but it failed commercially. It required more consumer research and was reintroduced in 1980 as Post-it Notes.

For references and additional reading, see Sources.

SECTION II

CHAPTER 4

Be Close to the Customer

People don't care how much you know until
they know how much you care.
—Theodore Roosevelt

We often focus on our competitors and worry about surprises from them, but more often than not, it is the customer who surprises us. Customer tastes and preferences can change quickly, sinking a promising business move. This is a particular problem for successful companies that believe their success is a vindication of their approach, and they continue on the same path even though the market has changed (i.e. Blockbuster).

So much has been written in the business literature about customer-facing, customer-focused, customer-centric business that some of the key underlying messages can get either taken for granted or lost in the ubiquitous drone. Very often, training or messaging takes a particular focus, such as customer service, customer product design, or customer marketing. But so often, when the rug is pulled out from under a company's plans, it is simply because it either doesn't know or has misread the customer. Given the wide and deep business literature on customer focus, there will be no attempt to repeat it here. Instead, we will simply paint the overall picture so that executives can frame their views of the customer, and we will offer some ideas for how to stay close to the customer.

Greg Shortell, president and CEO at Network Engines, talks about meshing corporate strategies with your customers. Perhaps a more complete way to look at that idea is the concept of finding a mutually beneficial relationship; in reality, you should both think of each other as partners, a marriage rather than a date. If you take advantage of your customer, you may make a short-term killing, but in the long term, you will lose them. Mutuality requires a shared relationship, shared goals, and will not take advantage or harm others. A mutual benefit will create a lasting relationship that doesn't require reselling constantly. And it is impossible to have a mutual benefit without understanding the needs of the other party; so, yes, you do need to have aligned strategies.

Focusing on the customer will allow your business to design products that really appeal to your consumers and organize around the service needs demanded by your customers. Many managers think they know the product, the industry, and the customer, and they go with what they are sure is correct instead of actually asking the customer. Back with the marriage analogy for the customer partnership—you know you should never assume what your spouse is thinking—talk to them and ask!

In his best-selling book, Carl Sewell reminds us that we have to ask the customer what they want. A good example of this is found in the quality standards pursued by M&M/Mars. The small colored candies usually don't last long enough between the package and your mouth to be closely examined by consumers, but the company has a fervent dedication to quality. In what could have been an overzealous commitment to quality, the candies were carefully examined to see if there were any cracks that could be found in the shells. This turned into reports, percentages, and engineering projects as any size or kind of crack was a clear defect and a violation of the high-quality standards established for the brand. However, if the customer gets to judge quality instead of the quality scientists in the ivory tower, you get a different answer. The customer really didn't care about the microscopic cracks in the candy. The quality scientists were barking up the wrong tree. Their assessment of quality did not match that of the customer. A key measure of knowing if you focus on the customer is asking, "Is the customer really boss—or do our experts know better?"

The well-known story of New Coke tells us some important things about following the consumer without fully understanding their motivations. In 1985, Coca-Cola released its famous New Coke product because it had been losing all the taste tests against the sweeter Pepsi, which Pepsi had made a key part of its advertising campaign. The consumer reaction was a tidal wave of resistance to the New Coke. Obviously, the Coke consumers did not want the sweeter product. Was there something invalid with the taste test? In fact, there was. When consumers drink a soft drink, they do not have a one-ounce sip. They usually drink a full twelve-ounce can or bottle. The impact of the sweetness is different on the palette with a twelve-ounce, fifteen-minute experience versus a one-ounce, three-second sip. The taste test gave data, but that data needed to be fully understood prior to a major reaction.

A similar story can be found with Hershey when they changed their iconic Hershey bar foil wrapper to a cheaper plastic wrap. A closely observed consumer would be seen playing with the foil wrap, folding and unfolding it into different shapes as they ate the product. The plastic wrap saved a lot of manufacturing money, but it changed the experience of consuming the product!

Sometimes, in a complicated business environment, there is so much data and so much changing at once that you can easily focus on the wrong thing: "You cannot see the forest for the trees." And this is what happened in the examples of Twix advertising and Snickers demand.

In the Twix advertising example, focus groups and data confirmed the effectiveness of the ad, but the definition of who the customer was became muddied. By focusing on the teenage customer (the tree), the decision makers missed the bigger picture (the forest). In the Snickers demand example, there was a lack of understanding about what drove the customer. The focus was on sales numbers and production. By not understanding why a customer purchased—and how they enjoyed—the product (the forest), the executives missed the important bigger picture, resulting in costly overproduction mistakes.

For references and additional reading, see Sources.

CHAPTER 5

Twix Advertising Won Awards but Lost Sales

A good decision is based on knowledge and not on numbers.

—Plato

Topics

- Customer awareness
- Conflicting objectives
- Complexity of data
- Use of data

Discussion Questions

- Is it better to pick a specific customer to satisfy than to try to satisfy all your customers—or even potential customers? Do some companies use one approach and some another?

- How can using data still give you the wrong answer?
- Can we get confused about the objective of a program (i.e. winning awards versus increasing sales)?

Twix was an up-and-coming brand at M&M/Mars. It was not in the same class as Snickers or M&Ms, and it didn't have the long history of Milky Way, but it was at the top of the second-tier brands and rapidly growing. The Twix marketing geniuses had what seemed to be a winning strategy.

Everyone knows that teenagers eat a disproportionate amount of candy and that teenagers like cutting edge and sometimes sarcastic humor. So, ads centered on appealing to teenagers were created. D'Arcy Masius Benton & Bowles Inc. was the agency that created the 1997 "Two for me, none for you" ad. This ad showed a Twix consumer considering whether to share the two pieces that came in a Twix bar and deciding that they would rather eat both themselves.

One showed a helpful Boy Scout doing his good turn by returning a lost Twix bar. The recipient said, "Thank you—you deserve a reward!" and proceeded to eat both pieces without sharing. Another showed a Frankenstein monster that wanted to share with a little girl, but he decided to part with one of his two arms instead of one of his two Twix pieces. Within the company, executives thought it was "fun" and "tongue-in-cheek." One agency insider said, "If you go out with the idea that you're not going to offend anybody, you probably won't make an impression" (Bloomberg).

The marketing folks at M&M/Mars knew they needed to be driven by data, and they ran focus groups to preview the ads before spending their money. This was standard procedure prior to any big spend, not just for the edgy ad being considered. The focus groups with teenagers came in with powerfully positive results, and the company proceeded to buy airtime targeted at teenagers. The ad was a success in many ways. *Adweek* picked it as one of its best spots of 1997. Marketing folks, especially the creative branch, love awards almost as much as the Hollywood stars. The controller within M&M/Mars was quoted telling the marketing folks, "We can't justify the spending based on awards—tell me what it will do to sales!"

And that became the problem. The more attention the ad got, the softer sales became. And then complaints started to materialize. Some folks cited the ad as an example of a loss of civility, as tasteless, as glorifying selfishness, and with an overall hostile message. There was even the thought that the iconic Boy Scout organization was being smeared. The impressions resulting from the ad and the soft sales were discussed at the highest levels of the corporate parent and even by the owners themselves. Mars had always been a very private and cautious company, and eventually, a decision was made to pull the ad.

How did a logical, data-driven decision that had all the right signals turn out to be so wrong? The answer can perhaps be found in a letter to *Adweek* from March 16, 1998:

I see you picked a Twix ad as one of your best of the year [Best Spots 1997, Feb. 2]. Because of the campaign's theme, I have chosen to never purchase my family's favorite candy bar again.

The "Two for me. None for you" tagline is catchy, but it teaches kids an attitude of selfishness, which I will not support. Mars lost my business with that one. From now on, my family will spend our money on Kit Kats (at least they give me a break!).

Janet Brister
Electronic marketing coordinator
AAPG Communications
Tulsa, Okla.

When the sales were analyzed, the fallacy in the logic became clear. While it was true that teenagers ate a disproportionate amount of candy, they only accounted for 15 percent of total purchases. Apparently, in successfully getting this small portion of purchasers excited, the ad had also ticked-off the other 85 percent, which is not a formula for success. This is quite similar to the problem politicians face when they appeal to their passionate base with messages that turn off the moderates and independents. The marketing decision makers had data—just not the total picture. So often, business executive only look at what they know and fail to pick up the whole picture. Sometimes, business executives only have limited data and have to go with it, but if so, they should proceed with great caution rather than overboard enthusiasm for the little bit of data they have. With limited data added to the complexity of the human environment, the probabilities of us being sure a certain event is "good" or "bad" become even smaller!

For references and additional reading, see Sources.

CHAPTER 6

The Five-Billion-Dollar Man

To succeed in business, to reach the top, an individual
must know all it is possible to know about that business.

—J. Paul Getty

Topics

- Industry expertise
- Corporate culture
- Change management

Discussion Questions

- If you are successful in one business or industry, will
  you be able to be successful in a different business or
  industry?

- After Mr. Nardelli took over, sales grew first—and then they fell. Why was there a different response over time to his changes?
- What would have possibly made Mr. Nardelli's tenure more successful long term?

During the summer of 2000, Home Depot had been quietly looking for a new chief executive. Only one of the three original founders, Arthur M. Blank, was still involved with day-to-day operations, and he wanted some help. The company's phenomenal recent growth and a slew of new challenges and strong competitors made it more and more difficult for Mr. Blank to handle the increasing demands. A search committee headed by Mr. Blank thought they had found the answer, but they would have to move quickly. GE's famous CEO, Jack Welch, was stepping down, and in the wake of naming his successor, two top underlings who had lost out in the competition to replace him, immediately generated a lot of attention as top candidates for CEO jobs elsewhere. Within nine days of the announcement that Immelt would replace Welch, both the losing candidates would end up accepting major jobs elsewhere. The Home Depot search committee moved quickly, but they had to, given the widespread interest in these runners-up.

Robert Nardelli, a hard-charging winner with more than twenty-five years at GE was named as president and chief executive officer of Home Depot. The news came after the close of stock trading for the day. That night, in after-hours trading, Home Depot shares rose $2.88 each for a staggering total market value gain of $5.5 billion. Mr. Nardelli, it seemed, was a five-billion-dollar man. To put in perspective this staggering vote of confidence, consider that the total net income Home Depot would earn in 2000 was $2.6 billion. Home Depot had moved quickly to seize an opportunity that they and the market believed would be good for their future. What do they say? If something is too good to be true, it probably isn't!

Mr. Nardelli had been one of GE's star performers and headed GE's Power Systems unit, a top-performing industrial unit within GE. Insiders told the *Wall Street Journal* that several board members favored him as the replacement for Jack Welch. Jack is quoted as saying, "He is the hardest-working guy you'll ever see." As a manager, he was known as demanding and someone who set high expectations but inspires his troops to the point that they would die for him.

Shortly after being hired, Mr. Nardelli's first communication through the annual report expressed excitement and respect for Home Depot's culture, its employees, and its past. He particularly emphasized outstanding customer service as the foundation upon which the business success had been achieved. He also made multiple references to the company's culture and expressed respect and appreciation for the strong culture. However, he had no background in retail, which only a few analysts raised as a concern.

Five years later, in a *Businessweek* article entitled "Renovating Home Depot," he was portrayed as a success, but a success who had changed the culture. He was credited with creating a *new* culture, not the one he had originally praised. The new culture was centralized and based on a military model, and it had three times the number of military veterans employed as did Walmart. Of the top 170 executives, 98 percent were new in their jobs since Mr. Nardelli's hiring, and many were hired from the outside. Whether or not this was good or bad could be debated, but it was surely different from the previous culture for which he had expressed respect and appreciation. However, it is obvious that you don't bring a hard-charging chief in just to keep everything the same.

Despite the change in culture, he was cast as a winner because sales had grown significantly, gross margin had also increased from 31 percent to 34 percent, and he had moved outside of retail to establish a strong presence in the wholesale supply chain to contractors.

What could not be debated was that there were some troubling signs. Despite the impressive performance numbers, the stock price was actually lower than when he had started six years earlier. One troubling harbinger was recent customer-service surveys. The University of Michigan Consumer Satisfaction Survey showed that Home Depot had fallen to last place among major retailers. If, in his first annual report, Mr. Nardelli was accurate about crediting strong customer service as the foundation upon which the past business success had been achieved, then that foundation had fallen apart. This was despite increased emphasis and measurement on customer service. The new culture had replaced all the "touchy-feely with military-style rule." There was increased emphasis on measurement and mechanics, but there seemed to be no soul and emotion in the effort, and what is customer service if not a human relation?

As a "do-it" kind of guy, Mr. Nardelli did accomplish many things at Home Depot. He invested more than a billion dollars in new technology related to self-checkout and inventory management. He diversified into wholesale and contractor supply. He brought in a new top management team and replaced many full-time workers at the stores with cheaper part-time workers. And he grew sales from $46 billion to $81 billion and doubled profits. A focus on cost management was needed at the previously easygoing Home Depot, and he instilled that mindset. However, he also apparently ticked off *all* his constituents! Customer-satisfaction scores were way down, employees lived in a shadow of fear, and even the stockholders had gone six years without any price improvement despite the impressive sales and profit growth. The kiss of death was the fact that, over the same six years, competitor Lowes's stock price went up by more than 200 percent.

Given no satisfied constituents, things got disagreeable when the ubiquitous business cycle began to take a toll. The housing slowdown in 2006 eroded the company's performance metrics, and stockholders would no longer accept Mr. Nardelli's massive $38 million compensation package given the lack of returns they had enjoyed. At a disastrous stockholder meeting in the spring of 2006, the board seemed to walk back their support.

When he was unwilling to make even a "symbolic adjustment" to his compensation plan, Home Depot and Mr. Nardelli parted ways. On January 3, 2017, the board announced their agreement. Interestingly enough, the stock price jumped 3 percent with the news, basically matching the euphoria seen when Mr. Nardelli was hired. So, he was a five-billion-dollar guy on both entrance and exit!

It turns out that the initial enthusiasm surrounding Mr. Nardelli's hiring was a little misplaced. The initial $5 billion vote of confidence dissipated, and when Mr. Nardelli left, the stock was no higher than when he started. The hiring committee gave Mr. Nardelli more than they had intended in order to attract him—even having Mr. Banks, a founder and the current CEO, step aside—because they were convinced this was a must-have opportunity. They celebrated the "good news" of his acceptance a little early. Good news, bad news—actually only time will tell. One must wonder if the aura surrounding GE at the time led them to their rapid and possibly not fully vetted decision. When a company whose culture was steeped in entrepreneurialism with a decentralized spirit brings in a hard-charging top-down control manager, you have to wonder why. They completed the hiring within nine days of Mr. Nardelli not receiving the top job at GE. Can you imagine the counsel you'd give one of your children who wanted to marry someone they only met nine days ago? Clearly the committee believed the opportunity was too good to pass up, and they jumped all over it, giving in to Mr. Nardelli's demands. Rapid decisions without the full due diligence process is one of the most common ways to turn a potential winning choice into a losing decision.

For references and additional reading, see Sources.

CHAPTER 7

Why You Want a Snickers Bar— Even If You're Not Hungry

Tell me what you eat and I will tell you who you are.

—Jean Anthelme

Topics

- Understanding the customer
- Building a business
- Supply chain management

Discussion Questions

- What are the costs associated with boom-and-bust sales performance?
- How can you stay close to the customer if they are on the other side of the globe (or the other side of town)?

Ed Lewis was the plant manager of the largest confectionary plant in the world. It was a position he had earned through years of managing high-performing teams. Toward the end of 1993, Ed looked over the Snickers production line. The line extended father than he could see, but the hustle of the workers to keep the line running smoothly was apparent everywhere he looked. When the line ran smoothly, it could churn out a million bars in a shift, and right then, every single one of those bars was needed. The recent demands for Snickers sales in Russia had exceeded all expectations, tapped out European production, and spilled over to the large plant in Texas.

Despite the pressure from corporate for more and more production, he was concerned. Ed knew that he could help, but it wouldn't be easy. He could add weekend shifts if he paid the workers time and a half, and he could run over the coming holidays using double-time pay. Certainly, some of his employees would appreciate the extra pay, but there were also concerns. Ed had the best interests of his workers at heart, and he knew that you could run your crew hard for a short time, but even the most dedicated workers would eventually need a break. Also, the maintenance crew was concerned about when they would be able to perform the required upkeep. Without the standard maintenance, there was the potential for something to go wrong, which could take an unacceptably large chunk out of production.

Ed was also getting some feedback from his financial crew that factored into his concerns. This level of production definitely raised costs. First, they were paying up to double time on labor for the extra production. Second, they had to source raw materials outside of the standard negotiated contracts—even bringing in some Chinese peanuts when the local sources dried up. Freight and transportation also were outside of the standard negotiated contracts and at higher spot rates. On top of all that, the product was being airfreighted all the way from Texas to Russia; how could that possibly be financially viable?

Snickers had just recently begun selling in Russia. Snickers was the first Western candy to be widely available and marketed in Russia. It was a huge success. Mars stated that its strategy was to grow rapidly so that a factory would be justified in Russia. As a result of a deep advertising program and the product available at kiosks on every corner, a $200-million factory was under construction as early as 1994. But Snickers became more than just a candy. It was a representation of Western-style economic reforms as represented by critics accusing President Boris Yeltsin of trying to "Snickerize Russia."

"Snickers is becoming a kind of a symbol," said Dmitri Ivliyev, consumer affairs reporter for the daily *Izvestia*. "Not only of Western life—I'd call it a symbol of our new times."

On the day after Christmas in 1991, the Soviet Union had officially ceased to exist. Despite the Russian economy being in a tailspin, trade possibilities immediately opened up with Russia along with market-determined prices. Along with the political changes and opening of trade, some of the other economic reforms were significant monetary reforms.

In the beginning of 1991, the USSR executed a significant and surprise monetary reform that withdrew 14 billion rubles from the economy, and then in 1993, Russia executed a major currency reform intended to tame inflation and exchanged notes for a new design. On July 24, 1993, the Central Bank of Russia announced the withdrawal of Soviet banknotes and their exchange for a new currency. As the economy collapsed with the withdrawal of central control and the huge reductions in military spending, private citizens scrambled for ways to survive. The inflation was more a result of the reduction in military production and an overall lack of product than an increase in currency. Unbeknownst to Ed and the production team in Texas, toward the end of 1993, these monetary and economic problems were actually a driving force behind the boom in Snickers sales. And what follows a boom? A bust.

And bust they did. After sales fell drastically, an investigation showed there had been hoarding of Snickers bars. Many of the Snickers bars sold were not eaten; they were saved. Just like prisoners of war used cigarettes as currency, Russia's nervous citizens were treating the Snickers bar, a symbol of Western life as money. The economic definition of money is something that can store value, something than can be used for exchange, and a unit of account. Snickers, which had a long shelf life and an easily recognized tamper-proof package, fit several of these definitions. And citizens, unable to get dollars, had been hoarding them as their personal safety net along with distributors and sellers.

By 1997, Russian attitudes had changed toward Western products. A cartoon made fun of Snickers using a tagline calling it the best antidote to hunger with an emancipated man who had starved to death. Consumers across the entire Eastern Bloc went fickle on foreign brands. Foreign companies were caught off guard, and for Mars, the peak of novelty hit in 1993 with sales declining over the next three years.

So, the sacrifices and extra costs that corporate demanded on Ed's Texas plant had probably been unnecessary, and in fact, the pumping up of sales probably lead to a harder fall. However, the early push for Snickers did build one of the first Western brands within Russia and led to a lasting presence and eventually a successful local manufacturing plant. Building a brand from scratch like that takes lots of investment, and perhaps the investment that the Texas plant had to make was only a marginal blip in the required initial losses. But, clearly, a better understanding of the consumer motivation would have mitigated some of the boom-and-bust cycle and saved significant operational costs.

For references and additional reading, see Sources.

SECTION III

CHAPTER 8

Focus on What You Can Control

If you don't know where you are going,
any road can take you there.
—Lewis Carroll

I remember being responsible for forecasting sales in a rice company. Occasionally we shipped a large cargo ship full of processed rice from the port of Houston. This could account for one fourth of the entire sales forecast for the month during which it occurred. Because the barges could not load and ship during a rainstorm, we had a number of forecasting failures simply because it rained during the last few days of the month, and the barges couldn't load as scheduled! It is one thing to offer the excuse, "I cannot control the weather," but what can management control? It was actually a simple option to incentivize the buyer to order in the second or third week of the month so that if it did rain, there was still time to load the barge and achieve the forecasted sales. Unbelievably, this problem had existed for years with complaints about the weather rather than managers looking at what they could control.

The inability to focus on things we can control is caused by complexity and uncertainty. The complexity of many of our operating environments can cause problems with management focus. While computers, robots, and technology have automated many tasks, there is no doubt that the quickening pace of business, global competition, government regulation, information overload, and rapidly change technology has made business more complex today than it was in decades past.

Because of uncertainty about the long term, businesses tend to focus on the short term. Companies shy away from long-term management in order to get short-term wins. Harvard Business School professor Bill George blames the financial crisis of 2008 on a culture of short-termism at the expense of long-term value. He quotes Warren Buffett as saying the best holding period is "forever." Especially in the short term, don't expect things to turn out like you planned. Owners and executives can get caught up with enthusiasm or despair over short-term results and lose discipline and direction.

Decisions that really build value are long-term decisions and require work over a longer period of time. Interestingly enough, there is more that we can do about long-term uncertainty than about short-term surprises, and so long-term uncertainly, while it may be greater, is more manageable than short-term uncertainty.

Excessive focus on short-term goals is a common problem, and an effort to overcome this issue was at the heart of the creation of the balanced scorecard. The balanced scorecard requires a company to review measurements from four different areas, including internal business processes, learning and growing, and customer as well as financial measures. The balanced scorecard requires that companies look at both leading and lagging indicators and internal and external ones. It is designed to include things that measure long-term and future progress instead of just historical financial performance.

I recommend a two-pronged approach for improving a business's ability to focus. First, have a strategic plan to direct your attention, and second, identify the critical success factors within your business.

Planning is a primary function of management. In its most basic form, it simply defines objectives and outlines a strategy for achieving them. When planning begins to take in more detail or focus on the shorter term, it will seek to obtain the necessary resources and align them appropriately. Planning is often much maligned as creating rigidity or attempting to replace management intuition. And while these criticisms are often deserved, at the high level outlined above, the planning function is an absolute necessity.

Every consulting group will have a process set up to help a business do a strategic plan, but unless it accomplishes a few key things, it has missed the boat:

- First, it should help the business to discover things about its potential that it didn't know
- Second, it should force strategic thinking so that a company can understand its opportunities and identify where focus will pay off.
- Finally, it should allocate and align resources.

This last point is particularly associated with the discussion here on focus. If there is an aligned focus on certain areas or projects on which resources will be extended, then all the confusion of a thousand competing issues, and the sure to arise uncertainty of an unstable world, should not distract the business into dead ends and alleys that it cannot control. When an airplane flies into a strong storm, it will be required to make many short-term adjustments, and as a business faces unknown challenges and unexpected changes, the situation is somewhat similar. Business plans at lower levels will require constant and major adjustments that are similar to a pilot's adjustment of the rudder, throttle, and other controls. However, the strategic plan is similar to the destination of the plane. Having a well thought out and agreed strategic plan allows the ship to make the necessary adjustments to stay on course. Imagine how a plane would behave in a terrible storm if it was uncertain of its destination!

For more than fifty years, the academic study of strategy has taught us that an organization's performance depends upon strong performance in a limited number of areas specific to the business/industry, which can be called *critical success factors*.

You don't have to be great at everything. A manager doesn't have to focus on everything; a manager can accept that many things are outside their control, but they do have to focus on and be good at a small list of very important priorities.

In the early 1980s, the executives at a leading confectionary company had planned a new product for Mexico, the Peso bar. This would be a well-known US candy bar of reduced size that would sell for exactly one peso. Price points had always been an important part of the confectionary business, partially because vending machines were an important distribution channel, and until recently, vending machines were tied to specific currencies and coins. Also price point was important because the range of snack products across which confectionary competes is very large (chips, drinks, cookies, nuts, etc.), and so perceived relative value was important. Manufacturing modifications were made on a line in Canada to provide this new bar, and additional investments in packaging design and advertising were made. However, just before the Peso bar launched, disaster struck when the dollar-peso exchange rate collapsed. There was no way the Peso bar could now be sold for a peso.

Management could not control the international exchange rate, and now they could not sell a bar for a peso. It would have been far better for them to target something they could control: value. They could still produce a product that could be seen as a good value for the Mexican consumer. This lesson has been seen multiple times. One recent example is the fast-food dollar menu. While it was an attractive marketing hook to call their special menu the "dollar menu," inflation saw to it that the name did not last long. Now the fast-food restaurants call their discount items a "value" menu or something similar. If managers focus on what they can control, they will not have to deal with as many unexpected surprises from the ever-changing business environment and the complex real world in which we operate.

A related example from this book is the story of Rockefeller and gasoline. When electrical lighting threatened his kerosene monopoly, he actually tried to fight it by convincing the public that electricity was dangerous. This was unsuccessful, but when he focused on what he could control—developing a good use for the by-product, gasoline—he then achieved his monumental success.

For references and additional reading, see Sources.

CHAPTER 9

The Worst Deal Ever Made

How to succeed: Try hard enough.
How to fail: Try too hard.
—Malcolm S. Forbes

Topics

- Structural market change
- Going big
- Corporate culture
- Reading the market

Discussion Questions

- How could two managers with so much success and so much capability make a decision that turned out to be so wrong? Did others see the problem?

- Many businesses fell prey to the internet bubble. What approaches could have brought sanity to the irrational expectations?
- Mr. Case claims the execution but not the vision was flawed; do you agree with him? How do we align execution with vision?
- When a business (AOL) that was based on a start-up mentality, with innovation, disruption, and risk gets big, even huge, how do the mindset and governance that previously led to its success need to change?

What kind of business deal would earn the moniker of worst deal ever made? At the time, couldn't analysts have seen the problems and avoided the deal? What could drive you with excitement over the cliff like that? Some business schools today study the AOL-Time Warner merger and call it the worst deal ever made. Yet this deal was conceived of and executed by some of the brightest high-tech minds and most experienced corporate executives.

Steve Case was an entrepreneur with an education in political science and a business background in marketing and brand management. He was the creator of AOL and a pioneering executive, and he was also a real nice guy. He led AOL, the leading internet company, and he had a vision for AOL to use its very high stock price to execute a merger. He was eager and willing to be aggressive. He felt the time of high stock prices was the time to strike.

Jerry Levin was a philosopher leader. He quoted from the Bible and ancient philosophers. He was the primary pioneer behind the creation of HBO. He had recently led Time Warner through difficult and often failed attempts to create its own internet presence. He and the board recognized the need to create distribution avenues that would work in the new digital world. In fact, that was the time, the height of the dot-com boom, when there was finally widespread acceptance that the internet would eventually be in every home and every business and would, given time, rule content distribution.

Steve Case was looking for opportunities. He wanted to go big—and Time Warner was the biggest—even though others had told him it could never happen. Steve and his wife were in China, a great opportunity to relax, but for someone like Steve, business was always on his mind. He saw other opportunities. He had a chance meeting with Levin and his wife in China, and a comfortable friendship emerged. The business opportunities soon began to fit into the conversations.

On January 10, 2000, the biggest merger of all time was announced. America Online Inc. would acquire Time Warner Inc. for roughly $182 billion in stock and debt. This was almost twice the price that Time Warner currently had on the market and would create a company with combined values of $350 billion. The deal would combine the world's number one internet provider and the world's top media company.

The excitement was almost universal. "Together they represent an unprecedented powerhouse. This alliance is unbeatable," said Scott Ehrens of Bear Stearns.

Steve Case said, "I don't think it is too much to say that

this really is a historic merger; a time when we've transformed the landscape of media and the internet!"

Time Warner President Richard Parsons said, "This is ... the pivotal moment in the unfolding of the internet age."

A lot of executives agreed that the merger was brilliant and worried about how their own companies would ever compete with the new giant.

The merger started off with a flurry of activity. AOL offered Time Warner's CNN.com, Entertaindom.com, and *InStyle* magazine on its service. Cross-promotion of AOL and the media products took place. However, these were all very small ideas and sidelines to the elements of critical success.

In the bigger picture, things did not go so well.

When the companies merged, Time provided 70 percent of the profit, but AOL actually controlled a greater stake of the combined company. This was due to the "inflated" price Wall Street was rewarding technology companies with during the high tech boom. This led to resentment on the Time Warner side.

Cultures were definitely a problem. Case wore dark business suits, and the Time Warner group usually went without ties. The Time Warner folks sometimes called the AOL group the "suits from Virginia." Even though the clothes were obviously not the problem, it was representative of the attitudes that led to the wardrobe selections. These conflicting attitudes were the problem. AOL was aggressive and arrogant, and Time Warner was a settled and sedate corporate culture.

Only two months after the deal was announced, the Nasdaq peaked and fell in what was called the dot-com crash.

The deal that had been originally listed at $350 billion was now valued at only $200 billion. All of a sudden, AOL was worth a whole lot less. On top of this, advertising revenues on the internet dried up. The AOL division was not growing, had less worth, and was generating less revenue. This exasperated the cultural conflicts, organizational confusion, and resentment.

AOL's standard dial-up service quickly became obsolete with the growth of high-speed internet. AOL went from an industry leader to a dinosaur in just a few short years.

In 2002, the SEC and Justice Department investigated AOL for inflating advertising revenues, an accusation first aired by the *Washington Post*. The company was forced to pay hefty fines and restate earnings. This could only exasperate the vitriol that many Time Warner employees felt toward their less than 50 percent stake in the company.

From the original $350 billion deal, the continuing struggles took a persistent toll on the new company's value. Seven years later, in 2009 (a market low), the combined companies were only worth $20 billion.

Many investors lost lots of money—but none more than Ted Turner. He lost $8 billion due to the declines in market value. The trail of despair included thousands of job losses, the loss of retirement accounts, investigations by the SEC and the Justice Department, and countless executive upheavals.

Today, Case quotes Thomas Edison when he says, "Vision without execution is hallucination."

For references and additional reading, see Sources.

CHAPTER 10

The Right Move with the Wrong Results

Based on the Case Write-up of James Harbin, PhD

Whatever you are, be a good one.

—Abraham Lincoln

Topics

- Power of a corporate vision
- Leadership
- Corporate culture

Discussion Questions

- How was Johnson's vision for J. C. Penney different from the previous direction? Which of these changes made sense, and which did not?

- How did shoppers respond to the new J. C. Penney?
- Did the changes that Johnson made take on a new set of competitors? How was J. C. Penney positioned against these new competitors?

J. C. Penney has a long history going back to its beginning in 1902 with a single store in a small Wyoming town. By the twenty-first century, it had truly become an American icon and a dominant force in the retail business. By 2011, the company had more than 1,100 stores, $17 billion in sales, and 160,000 employees (JCPenney, 2011), (Steffy, 2013).

Mr. Penney's stores were founded on "The Golden Rule," and as such, it was to a morally upright place to both work at and shop in (Reingold, 2012). A basic tenant of his philosophy was that great customer service made for a great brand. An often repeated and revered story was about the time Mr. J. C. Penney had brought in the manager of the most profitable store in his chain and chastened him for making too much profit. That manager obviously was not giving his customers a good deal.

But starting early in the 2000s, the company found itself struggling to find a niche in the retail apparel industry. Competition was heating up from both brick-and-mortar retailers to the quickly expanding internet industry. Penney's sales were stagnating; company stock was going nowhere, leaving shareholders unhappy. Many retail analysts and even their own customers, particularly the younger ones, often described the company as having evolved into one with a dowdy, stodgy, boring image.

The board of directors of J. C. Penney came under pressure to do something. There was a new, active, and very vocal member of the board by the name of William Ackman. He had earned his seat on the board as a result of acquiring 18 percent of the company stock. Mr. Ackman had a long history of being a "hedge fund guy," a wealthy individual who seeks to buy a large share in a company usually with the objective of using his influence on the board for a turnaround, hopefully resulting in the appreciation of his stock investment in the company. Hedge fund guys are sometimes correct in their choices of where to bet their money and influence, and sometimes, not so much. Mr. Ackman had previously made a big bet with Borders in 2006 before it went belly up (Steffy, 2013).

Mr. Ackman's opinion was that J. C. Penney needed a turnaround—and Ron Johnson was the guy to do it. Ron Johnson had a degree from Stanford and an MBA from Harvard. He also brought a proven track record of success at Apple as their vice president of retailing. He had worked directly under Steve Jobs. He had also recently served a short period of time as CEO of Target (Reingold, 2012).

The business story dominating the airwaves from late 2011 through 2013 revolved around the company, J. C. Penney, and the much anticipated arrival of their new CEO, Ron Johnson, his new vision for the company, and then the subsequent failure of that vision. It is a stark tale of how things can go from boom to bust in a short period of time. Early in Ron Johnson's reign, there was tremendous excitement among the financial community, the shareholders, and even the company itself. He took over the reins at J. C. Penney on November 1, 2011, and initially, his vision was given strong approval by the stock market with a price increase of more than 25 percent in just three months. How all that turned so quickly sour and ended in his dismissal eighteen short months later provides multiple lessons for understanding the uncertainty surrounding business decisions, especially when the conventional wisdom is claiming it is all good or bad.

Mr. Johnson was appointed CEO in late 2011 with a reputation as a maverick virtuoso of retailing based on his astonishing success pioneering the concept of Apple's retail stores. Johnson's vision for J. C. Penney was to transform its current boring image to one of being a cool place to shop. His strategy, formulated within a matter of days, included changing each of the company's 1,100 stores into a mini-mall concept. There were to be individual shops within each store. Each shop would be a lot more upscale as compared to what currently existed. These upscale shops would be designed to attract a higher-end customer. Some of the shops would even be leased—actually rented out to a high-profile designer company. J. C. Penney would be going after a different customer. Mr. Johnson was quoted as saying that J. C. Penney had the oldest customer base in retail (Reingold, 2012).

All those constant sales, discounts, and coupons that the company had come to depend on would be no more. The company had been conducting more than seven hundred different sales in a single year. It was Johnson's belief that customers would appreciate, and prefer, having an everyday fixed-value pricing approach over an everyday low-pricing strategy. Company employees were not even supposed to use the word "sale." That new strategy came while 75 percent of the company's present revenues were being generated by merchandise that had been discounted 50 percent or more. House brands, which were bringing in half of the company's revenues, were to be significantly scaled back under Johnson in favor of higher-priced name brands.

Typical of many turnaround specialists, Ron Johnson quickly surmised that the company had too many employees. Always a sure way of increasing stock price and igniting the financial community, pink slips were issued en masse. Almost twenty thousand J. C. Penney employees were terminated in his first twelve months as chief executive officer (Macke, 2014). This in a company where one of their values was loyalty, and even in the worst days of the 2009 recession, very few Penney employees were let go.

Ron Johnson brought in his own management team. Most of his new team was from outside the retail apparel industry. The new team also felt that the Plano headquarters had become "overstaffed and underproductive" (Bhasin, JCPenney COO, 2013). Johnson quickly moved to clean out the entire existing corner suite, and all the old senior team down through to the executive vice president and vice president levels were asked to leave. One-third of the 4,800 employees working at the company headquarters in Plano lost their jobs. One round of a 10 percent cut in personnel was referred to by the employees as "St. Valentine's Day Massacre" (Bhasin, Inside JCPenney, 2013). Many employees learned of their termination after being summoned to the Plano auditorium in groups of more than one hundred (Mattioli, 2013). The remaining long-term and previously loyal Penney executives were angered over rumors that the new team referred to the old team as "DOPEs: dumb old Penney employees" (Steffy, 2013) (Maheshwari, 2013).

The existing company logo was to be changed under Johnson. The Penney, from the existing J. C. Penney, was dropped in favor of the new "jcp" logo. Note the small-case letters like the "i" in iPhone. Maybe they should have taken a lesson from the GAP logo change and the furor it raised. Traditional company-wide pep rallies flew by the wayside. Additionally, Johnson did away with commissions for floor salespeople; he felt commissions interfered with quality customer service.

The new culture under Johnson became one of opacity—not transparency. There were few if any memos or written directives. Johnson kept many of his thoughts about Penney's new future close to the vest. Few details, if indeed there were any, were shared. Some likened it to the secretive environmental culture that existed at Apple. Few Penney employees knew what to expect next from Johnson and his team.

His personality was one that was hard to like. He has been described as egotistical, belligerent, insensitive, and one who would not accept excuses or no for an answer. Once he reached a decision, there was to be no wavering. Johnson once commented, several months into his strategy, "We have made the decision to change our pricing strategy, and we're going to stick to it" (Talley, 2012). A childhood friend had commented that what people loved the most about Ron Johnson, other than his talent, was his persistence; he was just relentless.

For the entire time that Johnson was CEO of J. C. Penney, he maintained his home in California. He jetted from Palo Alto to the company's headquarters in Plano, Texas, each week, and he stayed at the glitzy Ritz-Carlton hotel. Maybe it was not a big thing, but it probably conveyed a small but significant signal to those who worked in Plano. Some ex-executives of Penney said he rarely worked a full week while he was in Plano. His new number two, the president of the company, refused to move to Plano also, keeping his office in Minneapolis where he had been living (Bhasin, Inside JCPenney, 2013).

One longtime Penney executive commented, after working for a year under Johnson, that the "corporate culture had become very different" (Bhasin, Inside JCPenney, 2013). Another long-term executive said, "They (the new team) do not leave any opportunity for anyone to ask questions" (Bhasin, Inside JCPenney, 2013). One analyst was of the opinion that the company environment was becoming one of "Ron's way or the highway" (Bhasin, Deutsche Bank, 2012).

Ron Johnson's tenure at J. C. Penney lasted a brief seventeen months (late 2011 until early 2013). The board asked for his resignation in April 2013. Net sales fell more than 24 percent from more than $17 billion in 2011 to $12 billion in 2012. Along with lower sales, the company also posted a stunning loss of $1.38 billion (JCPenney, 2013). The company stock plummeted from above $40 a share when Johnson started to less than $10 a share when he left (Table 2). The company's workforce had been cut by more than forty thousand during Johnson's tenure. Adding insult to injury, Ron Johnson was awarded the "Motley Fool's Worst CEO of the year" in late 2013 (Williams, 2012).

In the end, the company paid out more than $236 million in executive compensation to Johnson and his team. In return, the company had nothing to show for it except billions in lost sales, thousands of loyal customers gone, a store remodeling program only just begun, a badly demoralized workforce, and worst of all, a mortally wounded American icon. Was it Ron Johnson's vision that was flawed—or the execution of that vision? The vision itself, along with Mr. Johnson's previous success, is the thing that created initial enthusiasm in the market. But a vision that cannot be executed is only a dream and is not worth the initial excitement that was generated.

Chapter 10, "The Right Move with the Wrong Results," is based on the case write-up of James Harbin, PhD. It is used with his permission.

For references and additional reading, see Sources.

SECTION IV

CHAPTER 11

Concluding Thoughts

There are talkers enough among us; I'll be one of the doers.
—Charles Dickens

Since every company will face surprises and change, it should face this imperative as an opportunity to drive the business to new heights instead of causing it to crash and burn like Blockbuster and Kodak. In order to do so, it must adapt, properly and strategically—as outlined in the sections on staying flexible, being close to the customer, and focusing on what you can control.

Even if executives understand these issues, it is also critically important that your people also understand. William Faulkner said, "You have to learn to kill your darlings." Sometimes being attached to what we like or think works instead holds us back. Some people associate change with loss and resist or block change. The key to a company being able to adapt to change is the people within the company. The associates need to thrive in the midst of change. Indeed, in his book *Good to Great,* Jim Collins wrote, "A company should limit its growth based on its ability to attract enough of the right people."

An example of giving up "darlings" to allow for change was demonstrated in the small city of Orem, Utah. For years, Orem relied heavily upon a large steel mill as its economic engine. Like many American heavy industries, this steel mill was struggling and uncompetitive with the newer, more efficient factories. City managers forecasted dire results if the stressed steel mill closed, and many local resources were dedicated to try to keep the steel mill running and employing the locals.

Eventually, reality took over, and the steel mill was forced to close. What happened? Was there large unemployment and economic turbulence? If any, it was only for a very short time. The hole created when the steel mill closed actually provided a great opportunity for many modern and up-and-coming businesses to move in and use the available local labor and resources to succeed, and they have thrived. Today, the city has a very successful broad-based economy with high tech, health care, education, and light manufacturing. This could never have happened if the city continued to cling to the dying steel mill.

Staying Flexible

A great example of providing necessary reserves in advance of great risk is Ford's ability to avoid taking government TARP funds. When GMC and Chrysler LLC faced bankruptcy in 2008, Ford did not, although its business situation was just as dire. Ford was in better shape than the others because it had mortgaged its assets in advance of the financial crisis to raise $23.6 billion. The loans were used to retool its product lineup to focus on customer desires for smaller, energy-efficient vehicles. It got the United Automobile Workers to agree it could finance half of a new retiree health care trust with company stock. By April 2009, it retired $9.9 billion of the debt it had taken out in 2006. Ford's ability to forgo the TARP funding provided it more control of its operations and gave it a huge public relations victory with the car-buying public.

COVID-19 provides another example of the need for flexibility and the associated problems with forecasting. No one was forecasting a worldwide pandemic and country-wide full-scale economic shutdowns. Sanjay Sehgal of KPMG said, "COVID-19 has shattered all forecasting models. No one is going to be able to create perfect forecasts right now. But companies that incorporate external signals into their modeling and harness the power of artificial intelligence will definitely come out ahead."

Airlines, hotels, and restaurants immediately saw the majority of revenue end. Governments forced shutdowns of many businesses. Other companies (bike sellers, Amazon) saw large, unexpected increases in business. Whatever the forecast had been, it was now worthless. The ability to update the forecast, while critical, was also almost impossible due to the unknowns. However, finding a plausible path forward was not impossible.

Companies could chart a variety of options and associated probabilities for potential paths. Finding sources of short-term funding became critical—just weeks after everything was going well for many of these companies. Communication with investors, bankers, and customers was required at exponential levels of what it had been just weeks before. While many businesses slowed down and laid off employees, the management teams were forced to double their efforts and explore new ways and options if they didn't just want to accept the hands they had been dealt.

One company that arguably handled the challenges of COVID-19 as well as possible was a hospitality company that sold memberships in private vacation homes around the world. When travel was shut down and people were forced to quarantine, their business was basically put on hold. One month before the European and American shutdowns started, one of their board members who was well connected in global circles warned the board that the situation was going to get very bad. As a result, the company prepared plans A, B, C, and D in advance of the business disruption. Plan A addressed minor business interruptions, and then each succeeding plan gave options to address more and more difficulties. Some of these executives had worked through the challenges of the

Great Recession and 9/11. As a result, they knew how much advanced preparation helped them. The impact of COVID-19 was catastrophic for this company. In fact, they blew through these four plans in several months and quickly had to create some new ones.

As part of implementing these plans and navigating the choppy waters, the board of directors met weekly, and the executive staff held daily company-wide communications. Of course, these plans were not easy; they involved layoffs, reduced salaries, and negotiations with lenders and customers. However, they also provided the necessary flexibility and instilled the confidence in customers, employees, and other stakeholders to ride out the worst of the problem. This company also focused on the customer (who paid yearly subscriptions) with personal communication. They were effective in keeping most customers in the program and paying their membership dues despite the interruptions. This company also focused on what it could control. For example, on cash management, they worked where they had leverage, and they built individual arguments for negotiations with each lender and leaseholder to position reduced or slower payments. While this company still has many challenges ahead, things were looking up for them by November 2020.

Another company, which has successfully transitioned its business in the face of unexpected shocks, is Orsted, a Danish energy company. In the summer of 2008, natural gas prices cratered, dropping 78 percent in two months. If you were a natural gas company, how would you respond?

Orsted saw a future in its very small offshore wind farm. Over the past decade, with significant investment, it has now completed a major shift to offshore wind electrical generation. The company, which supplies 49 percent of Danish electrical production and has set up offshore windfarm operations in the United States, has now completely divested itself of its once core oil and gas operations.

In transition periods, having that end goal from a flexible planning process is critical. That goal can keep you moving the rudder correctly as you navigate the turbulent river current.

Stay Close to the Customer

Staying close to the customer is really like navigating turns on a trip. The customer road is not straight, and it will have many turns, some which come up quickly and are sharp hard turns to make. However, if you do not make the turns, you will find yourself completely off the road!

With COVID resulting in restrictions on gatherings, working, and learning from home, Zoom has suddenly become the go-to provider instead of the previous mainstay Skype. We are all Zooming now, and Skype missed the turn. For a while, Skype had not been responding to customers, which opened up the landscape for competitors like Zoom. Skype was sold to eBay, then went private, and then was acquired by Microsoft. Skype had three different owners in six years. Skype took multiple and varied direction from these three owners rather than taking direction from the consumer. Skype's quality deteriorated, and it was unbearably buggy and full of spam. Consumers wanted simple, easy, and no spam! Zoom provided two major advantages; it was so simple that even non-tech schoolkids could use it without support, and all you needed to join a meeting was an email! The market value of zoom has increased ten times over eight months during the pandemic.

Staying close to the customer keeps you from going off the road, and it can give you great direction and new ideas for the future. Ecolab transitioned from selling industrial cleansers and food-safety services by talking to its customers. The same customers who were buying its core products were also voicing concerns about access to clean water. Ecolab acquired water technology company Nalco, and they are now one of the world's leading providers of efficient water solutions. If you understand the customer, you know what they need and how to service them!

Focus on What You Can Control

The final element of this book's three-pronged approach is focusing on what you can control. It is more than a mantra for personal life success; it is critical for companies. Steve Maraboli, a behavioral scientist, said, "Incredible change happens in your life when you decide to take control of what you do have power over instead of craving control over what you don't."

For more than fifty years, the academic study of strategy has taught us that an organization's performance depends upon strong performance in a limited number of areas that are specific to the business or industry, which are *critical success factors*. You don't have to be great at everything. A manager doesn't have to focus on everything—a manager can accept that many things are outside their control—but they do have to focus on and be good at a small list of very important priorities. Businesses cannot control the economy, their customers or competitors, the weather, or even most trends and fashions. They can control their business processes, their price, value, quality of product and service, and where they invest in people, R&D, and equipment.

While at M&M/Mars, I observed how many executives were obsessed with watching our competitors. Would they raise prices? Would they launch a product in a specific category? Would they load the trade at year-end? While competitive information is key to planning, being prepared, and executing responses, we could only focus on our own price (value proposition) and our own new product launches.

A great example of focusing on what you can control was shown in our policy for accounts payable collection from our customers. When a customer goes bankrupt, they don't pay you, and if they are a major customer, the problem can be very expensive. Standard payment policy within the industry was "2/10 net 30," meaning that if paid within ten days, a 2 percent discount was permitted. We could control the payment terms, and the 2 percent discount was an incentive to ensure we collected our payments in a timely fashion. After much debate and discussion, we changed the terms to "3/5 net 30," which was unique in the industry. While it did cost M&M/Mars an additional discount to get the payment earlier, we found it was worth it. When major customer Kmart went bankrupt, our competitors were out a lot of money. We however, had been paid, with the exception of a very minor amount. We could not control Kmart's bankruptcy, but by focusing on what we could control, we got our money early and came out ahead.

Netflix CEO Reed Hastings said, "We don't and can't compete on breadth with Comcast, Sky, Amazon, Apple, Microsoft, Sony, or Google. For us to be hugely successful, we have to be a focused passion brand. Starbucks, not 7-Eleven. Southwest, not United. HBO, not Dish." What could they control? Original content. Hastings asked for original content that could win Emmys and Oscars. In 2020, Netflix received twenty-four Oscar nominations—more than any other media company. Netflix had two pictures nominated that year for best picture, *The Irishman* and *Marriage Story*. In 2020, Netflix also dominated the Emmys with 160 nominations. Has this strategy of focusing on what you can control worked? Netflix's stock price has gone from 18.57 to 51.65 (+178 percent) in the past five years.

The takeaway lesson from all of this is obvious—companies can survive and prosper when faced with change if they are willing to be flexible, concentrate on and understand the customer, and focus on what they can control.

For references and additional reading, see Sources.

SOURCES

Chapter 1: Stay Flexible

Meier, J.D. 2010 *Getting the Results the Agile Way,* Innovation Playhouse, LLC.

Saffo, P. 2007, "Six Rules for Effective Forecasting," *Harvard Business Review*, July 2007.

KPMG, "Forecasting with Confidence, Economist Intelligence Unit." KPMG.com.

Gallo, A. "Keeping Your Business Plan Flexible," *Harvard Business Review,* September 2, 2010.

Reeves, M. and Deimler, M. "Adaptability: The New Competitive Advantage," *Harvard Business Review*, August 2011.

Chapter 2: Turning Waste to Gold

Chernow, R. *Titan,* Vintage Random House, Inc., New York.

Wikipedia: John D. Rockefeller.

Wikipedia: Wars of currents.

"History of gasoline," US Energy Information Administration.

"Henry Ford Biography," Biography.com.

Cline, B. "The History of Kerosene," *History Magazine* August/September 2007.

Snodgrass, M. E. *The Civil War Era and Reconstruction: An Encyclopedia of Social, Political, Cultural, and Economic History*, Routledge, 2015.

"Free Alcohol Hearings," House Ways & Means Committee, 113

Brough, J. *The Ford Dynasty: An American Story*, 118.

Chapter 3 An Idea without a Home

3M brand page http://www.post-it.com/3M/en_US/post-it/contact-us/about-us/.

Wikipedia https://en.wikipedia.org/wiki/Post-it_note.

Donnelly, Tim. "9 Brilliant Inventions Made by Mistake" *Small Business,* www.aabacosmallbusiness.com/advisor/9-brilliant-inventions-made-by-mistake.html.

Bellis, M. "Post-It Note," *About Money,* about.com. http://inventors.about.com/od/pstartinventions/a/post_it_note.htm.

Jaruzelski, B., Holman, R., and Baker, E. "3M's Open Innovation," *Strategy+Business,* 2011, http://www.strategy-business.com/article/00078?gko=121c3.

Huang, R. "Six Sigma Killed innovation at 3M," *ZDNet.* 2013, http://www.zdnet.com/article/six-sigma-killed-innovation-in-3m/.

Chapter 4: Be Close to the Customer

James, Geoffrey. "Be Customer-Focused," Inc.com, November 6, 2012.

Gottfredson, Mark and Markley, Rob. *Focus on the Customer*, Bain Insights, Bain & Company. Aug. 13, 2014.

Sewell, Carl and Brown, Paul. *Customers for Life*, Crown Business, 2009.

Miller, Ray and Miller, Laura. *That's Customer Focus!*, Book Surge Publishing, 2008.

Chapter 5: Twix Advertising Won Awards but Lost Sales

Adweek, March 16, 1998.

Bloomberg Business, "Gen X ads: 'Two for me, none for you,' August 10, 1997.

Chapter 6: The Five-Billion-Dollar Man

Grow, B. "Tough as Nails!," *Businessweek*, March 6, 2006.

Grow, B. Blowup at Home Depot, *Businessweek*, January 15, 2007.

Home Depot Annual Reports.

Lublin, J, Murray, M. Brooks, R. "Home Depot Names GE's Nardelli as New CEO in Surprise Move," *Wall Street Journal,* December 6, 2000.

Kavilanz, T. "Nardelli out at Home Depot," CNN Money, January 3, 2007.

Chapter 7: Why You Want a Snickers Bar—Even If You're Not Hungry

Wikipedia Monetary Reform in the Soviet Union, 1991 and 1993.

Troitsyna, M. "Soviet Ruble Was Destroyed Brutally in One Day," Pravda.ru, July 24, 2013.

McKay, B. "Mars Inc. Finds Russia Nothing to Snicker At," *Advertising Age*, November 21, 1994.

Goldberg, C. "A Sweet and Nutty Craze Hits Russia," *Los Angeles Times,* January 21, 1994.

Williamson, E. "Russians Getting Sweet on the Nation's Candy," *Chicago Tribune*, November 23, 1997.

Chapter 8: Focus on What You Can Control

Kaplan, Robert S. "Conceptual Foundations of the Balanced Scorecard," *Harvard Business Review*, working paper 10-074.

George, Bill. "Focus on the Short-Term Hurts Companies," *Wall Street Journal*, October 29, 2009.

Chapter 9: The Worst Deal Ever Made

Johnson, Tom. "That's AOL, folks." CNNMoney, January 10, 2000.

Weissman, Cale. "Steve Case on AOL-Time Warner: I don't regret doing the merger." *Pando*, April 3, 2014.

Hu, Jim. "AOL to Buy Time Warner in High-Stakes Merger," *CNET*, August 10, 2005 (reprint).

McCracken, Harry. "The 2000 and 2015 AOL Merger Press Releases: Compare and Contrast," Fastcompany.com, 2015.

Arango, Tim. "How the AOL-Time Warner Merger Went So Wrong," *New York Times,* January 10, 2010.

McGrath, Rita. "15 years later, lessons from the failed AOL-Time Warner merger," Fortune.com January 10, 2015.

Benner Katie (2015) "Lessons from the AOL-Time Warner Disaster," BloombergView, January 14, 2015.

Chapter 10: The Right Move with the Wrong Results

JCPenney. (2012, January). J.C. Penney, Inc. 2011 Annual Report. Retrieved August 20, 2014, from JcPenney: http://www.jcpmediaroom.com/annual-report.

Macke, J. (2014, January 16). "Breakout." Retrieved January 16, 2014, from Yahoo Finance: http://finance.yahoo.com/ blogs/breakout/j-c--penney-to-cut-2-000-jobs-and -close-33-stores--what-does-it-mean-for-customers- 155453366.html;_ylt=AwrBT9CqSDlUF4cAXj BXNyoA;_ylu=X3oDMTEzbG1oMjgxBHNlYw NzcgRwb3MDMQRjb2xvA2JmMQR2dGlkA 1ZJUDUwNF8x.

Maheshwari, S. (2013, March 21). "JCPenney High Flying Executives." Retrieved March 21, 2013, from Bloomberg Businessweek: http://www.businessweek.com/news/2013-03-20/j-dot-c-dot-penney-plane-commute-executives-seen-hurting-revamp#p2.

Mattioli, D. (2013, April). "Penney Wounded by Deep Staff Cuts." Retrieved April 15, 2013, from Yahoo Finance: http://finance.yahoo.com/news/Penney-wounded-deep-staff-cuts-0019.

Reingold, J. (2012, March 19). "Retail's New Radical," *Fortune*, 125–131.

Steffy, L. (2013, January 4). "Unlucky Penney." *Texas Monthly*, 54+.

Task, A. (2012, May 10). "The Daily Ticker." Retrieved June 21, 2012, from Yahoo Finance: http://finance.yahoo.com/blogs/daily-ticker/j-c-penney-sears-ron-johnson-done-incalculable-160736591.html;_ylt=AwrBT8SvUjlUMGQAUflXNyoA;_ylu=X3oDMTEzbG1oMjgxBHNlYwNzcgRwb3MDMQRjb2xvA2JmMQR2dGlkA1ZJUDUwNF8x.

Williams, S. (2012, December 12). "The Motley Fool's Worst CEO of the Year Is ..." Retrieved December 12, 2012, from The Motley Fool: http://www.fool.com/investing/general/2013/12/12/the-motley-fools-worst-ceo-of-the-year-is-2.aspx.

Chapter 11: Concluding Thoughts

Anthony, S., Trotter, A. and Schwartz, E. "The Top 20 Business Transformations of the Last Decade," *Harvard Business Review,* September 24, 2019.

Addante, F. 2016, "Why the Best Companies Embrace Constant Change," INC.com July 26, 2016.

Amadeo, K. and Estevez, E. 2020, "Auto Industry Bailout," The Balance.com.

Sanjay Sehgal, KPMG LLP. "Covid-19 and the CFO," April 2020.

ABOUT THE AUTHOR

Richard Parsons has had senior-level executive experience with some of the largest and most well-known companies in the world. Among other responsibilities, he was corporate controller for M&M/Mars. He earned a Ph.D. in economics and is on the faculty at Texas A&M University – Texarkana, where he teaches and researches. He has taught business planning, business strategy, business forecasting, economics, and finance. An avid skier and birdwatcher, he can be reached at drrichardparsons@gmail.com.

CPSIA information can be obtained
at www.ICGtesting.com
Printed in the USA
LVHW092019230721
693398LV00014B/431